Learning NLP Through Self-Coaching

Understand, learn and develop neurolinguistic programming with powerful NLP techniques - easily explained with exercises and examples

by Paul Edelmaier

Table of Contents

1. Introduction

Society is inconceivable without communication. But many wrong approaches to communication are possible. Misunderstandings, disputes and lack of development are among the consequences of this wrong communication. The three letters "NLP" have been appearing increasingly in this context for several years. But NLP is not only connected with communication, it is also very strongly associated with selective perception. But what exactly is behind it and how can entrepreneurs, salespeople, pupils, students and employees benefit from it? The secret is the techniques of NLP and the possibilities of neurolinguistic programming.

Now, of course, you have the opportunity to attend one of the numerous seminars on NLP and develop further. For a change such a step is often not necessary at all. NLP is a useful instrument in self-coaching and is suitable for personal development. In the following pages you will find out exactly what NLP is all about. Suitable exercises and structures for big changes according to the system are also possible. As with any approach to personality development, sufficient patience and consistency in the exercises are important. In this way you will never see communication the way it was before.

The techniques described in this book will also help you to discover your own personal resources. Promoting these is an essential part of the following exercises. For a better implementation in everyday life, you will find practical examples that show exactly how the techniques can really be used. After all, success can only be expected if the techniques are applied appropriately and not if the NLP techniques are only applied half-heartedly. With a little patience and the will to change something, you can develop your personality with NLP in self-coaching for positive change. For a better insight you will find in this book not only one but several popular NLP techniques. This also makes it easier to discover exactly the right technique for optimal success.

In this book you will learn:

- to discover and release your resources.

- how to recognize, use and transform your personal, selective perception.

- how to trigger feelings with certain triggers or anchors.

- to solve blockages.

- to understand and then let go of negative feelings in certain situations.

- to get to the bottom of the causes of your attitudes and feelings.

2. What does "NLP" mean?

The abbreviation NLP stands for Neuro-Linguistic Programming. In short, it is an interesting collection of communication techniques. In addition, there are methods in NLP that can change mental processes in humans. These methods or rather techniques originate from different forms of therapy of mentally ill people, which are supposed to change something profoundly. The forms of therapy used include Gestalt therapy, hypnotherapy and cognitive techniques. Only one of many techniques of NLP are linguistic images or the timeline. You will get to know these techniques even better in the following course and can then use them for yourself.

In order to understand NLP and the associated possibilities it makes sense to take the term apart. Then the coming techniques will be more understandable. NLP contains the terms neuro, linguistics and programming. But how are these terms to be understood exactly?

Neuro is a common abbreviation of neurology. Neurology is the science of the nervous system. With our nerves, or rather sensory organs, we also absorb information from our surroundings. The nervous system is therefore responsible for our exact perception. How exactly we think, feel and act depends on the perception and processing of the information by the nervous system. But it can also be concluded directly from this that perception is a subjective matter because each person's nervous system is different and the perception of the same thing is therefore different for two people. This point leads to the assumption that for this reason the perception is also controllable.

Another important term in NLP is linguistics. Linguistics generally refers to the language used to communicate with other people. Linguistics is therefore the teaching of language. There is definitely not only one way of approaching language; there are many linguistic means that lead to different goals. Surely you know good salespeople and those who may not be able to convince by the choice of their language. The same applies to teachers, professors, managers and everyone else. Because the linguistic means are manifold it definitely makes sense to deal with these means for more success in life. But linguistics does not only mean linguistic communication with the people in the surrounding area. Rather, linguistics also refers to inner communication with oneself. We can use a pictorial language within ourselves and the linguistic internal communication has a great influence on the external effect.

This means, for example, the sentence: "I am beautiful," or "Next year, I'll lie on the beach with a flat stomach in swimsuits." In this way we influence ourselves and paint pictures inside ourselves. These statements and pictures create a positive or negative impression. Those who always only think, *I am ugly*, feel themselves to be ugly. And many other people have the same impression due to the very unattractive charisma. With these words you can create your own reality inside as well as design it. Linguistics thus represents an important starting point for changes in communication, both externally and internally.

Last but not least, neurolinguistic programming is also known as programming. This term is not only used for the use of electronic devices. Rather, one's own subconscious mind can also be programmed, as can behavioral patterns. In this respect, programming means a permanent, systematic change. Therefore

NLP aims at targeted and permanent changes in communication and perception. This allows you to discard unwanted behaviors, take targeted action against problems and also achieve better communication. This is an advantage in many areas of life and certainly not only as a salesperson. In addition, the combination of NLP with self-coaching represents a particularly interesting approach. This way you will learn appropriate techniques and not least go on a journey to your inner self.

The whole system was developed in the '70s in the USA because John Grinder and Richard Bandler asked themselves what successful therapists do differently than all the others. They were looking for special techniques and procedures with which success in therapy is particularly likely. Trying out, observing and systematically implementing them therefore led to the original NLP. These original assumptions have been greatly expanded over the past decades, so that today it is rather a collection of methods. The subjective perception of people always forms the basis and is the point at which NLP starts. In addition, the visual, inner imagination is of great importance in the exercises and is indispensable for their implementation.

3. Self-coaching and the journey to your own self

Again and again in recent years speech is of self-coaching. Similar to meditation or yoga, self-coaching is one of the things that can lead to changes in personality. More calmness, calmness and inner strength are the consequences of correct application. Self-coaching with the right techniques represents a journey to one's own self. Furthermore, with the right techniques it is possible to reprogram certain practiced behavioral patterns on a long-term basis. With a coach you can achieve very good results with the appropriate cooperation. But the question is rather what happens if you don't find a suitable coach for your needs. But this is exactly what can happen and is very often the case in reality.

The option of self-coaching is therefore rightly gaining more and more popularity, as interesting changes are also possible. Self-coaching is about reflecting you without the help of an external coach. This self-reflection takes place with the help of certain techniques that are clearly defined. It should be noted that self-coaching sometimes comes up against criticism. Critical voices say that a coach is always necessary for the development of coaching. Without the thought impulses from outside it is not possible, according to critics, to develop itself further. Rather nothing happens then at all because one turns ever further in the circle. That's what critics say. But very many humans have had success with Selbstcoaching and obtain self-reflection and purposeful argument with their own behaviors and problems and achieve considerable progress. NLP aims exactly at that in the Selbstcoaching. A coach can also mediate NLP. But the attempt to try it with the techniques and to cause such a change is likewise interesting. Basically, self-coaching aims to achieve something in private as well as in professional life with certain techniques and exercises. The development of one's own personality without outside help is therefore clearly in the foreground.

3.1 The importance of communication in everyday life

But why exactly does it make sense to try so hard to communicate? It should be noted that we humans always and everywhere communicate with our environment. No matter whether things are spoken or not, communication is always present. Precisely because communication is simply part of it and it is impossible not to communicate at all, it represents a good approach to change. And communication and the improvement of communication is what NLP is all about. We communicate verbally and non-verbally all the same time with our environment and ourselves. The critical voice in your head? It's just as much about communication as it is about talking to friends or keeping quiet about a beggar. However, communication takes place on different levels.

The term communication comes from Latin and is derived from the word communicatio. It is therefore a matter of communication in spoken, written or silent form. The last option takes place through facial expressions, gestures and the entire posture as well as through the tone of voice. Through communication, we can get stuck in a lot in everyday life, but at the same time we can also achieve a great deal if we use it correctly. It is therefore a matter of optimizing and understanding communication and also understanding the reactions to one's own statements. To influence these is important for every salesperson, no matter in which branch or at which age. Because who knows how he can influence his interlocutors; it may lead to the possibility to change his reaction. But one reacts also—to statements, pictures, smells or songs—and communication is not always in such a way as to be best for the goal. Communication is therefore an important tool and a great resource that has not yet been fully exploited by most people. NLP deals on the one hand exactly with this communication and on the other hand with the techniques to influence one's own reaction exactly like the reaction of others.

3.2 Use of NLP and the possibilities in self-coaching

NLP is therefore about changing certain behaviors and communication for the positive. Since NLP is a method derived from therapy, there are also principles that are important for understanding. The principles or paradigms are just as important as the guidelines presented below. It simplifies the application of the individual techniques if you familiarize yourself with the guidelines and think about them briefly. Basically, it is important that people's inner perception, as explained above, is related to sensory perception. The interesting thing is that every human being has one or two sensory organs, which he prefers to perceive. To use all senses equally would be rather difficult and overwhelming. The distinction between visual and non-visual types is therefore no accident. Therefore, take a short look at the five senses and consider best which senses are particularly important for you. Surely you have one or two senses that are more important for your perception than others.

The perception of man is based on the **five senses:**

- Eyes: Visual perception with the eyes that are also called the sense of sight.

- Ears: Auditory perception with the sense of hearing.

- Sense: Also known as Kinesthetic or Sense. Perception through the skin with all parts of the body.

- Olfactory sense: Olfactory perception through the nose.

- Sense of taste: Gustatory perception with the sense of taste, i.e. with the tongue and the pharyngeal mucosa.

But now every human being uses his senses differently and therefore absorbs his surroundings in his own way. This means, for example, that a song can evoke different emotions depending on its character or experience. This realization is important for the further procedure and helpful with regard to the coming exercises. Basically NLP is not a single method but rather a collection of techniques. This is exactly what sets NLP apart from other forms of therapy and it is also not a scientific method. The different schools and points of view lead to the fact that an entire treatise on NLP is very difficult. Rather it makes sense to always select individual aspects. However, the following 12 guidelines are decisive and appear again and again in connection with NLP exercises with the guidelines that are in any case possible in self-coaching.

4. Guiding principles of considerations around NLP

There are some important guiding principles that determine NLP and they should therefore also be used in the context of self-coaching. These guidelines have proven their worth and will help you to slowly work on your problems and develop further. The guidelines also include exercises and techniques that you can apply. It makes sense to always use only the methods that are suitable for you because not every guiding principle is interesting for you at the moment. In the following pages you will learn some of these guiding principles, which can also be very well integrated into exercises. The knowledge of the guidelines is helpful, especially for the initial understanding of NLP and its possibilities. Without the guidelines it is sometimes quite difficult to understand what NLP is all about. The assumptions are therefore a basis for self-coaching as well as for cooperation with an external coach.

The well-known guiding principles are:

1. The map is not the area

Later you will learn more about the personal maps, which play a very important role in NLP. In short, a map is a very personal affair, determined by past experiences. The map is an inner construction and ensures that people have a certain reaction to a situation. For example, a woman who was previously cheated on by her partner has a different map in a corresponding situation than a woman who has never been confronted with cheating. It is a kind of reality of people that does not correspond to the real reality and helps to act in individual situations. There are also no right or wrong maps. However, there are useful and not-so-useful maps in NLP so that they can be changed and adapted. The first principle says that this inner map does not correspond to the actual area because it is a subjective perception.

2. People always make the best possible choice for them

Now you can call this behavior selfish or just plain normal. The point is that people always give their best and make the best choice according to their history, their experiences and their perception. On the outside, this choice may seem negative, but from a human perspective it is the best decision. This is not only helpful in NLP but also when it comes to communication. One is not in the skin of the other and therefore also does not know why exactly the acting turns out in such a way or which history is exactly behind this acting.

3. Every behavior has a positive intention

The third guiding principle fits or complements the second guiding principle. People always do what is best for them and do these things out of positive motivation. Behind every behavior is a positive and not a self-destructive intention. The interesting thing about this assumption is that positive intention often has to be fathomed first. An often used example is an overweight person who still continues to eat. Why exactly does he keep eating, even though he feels uncomfortable and should and should lose weight? This can be due, for example, to a protective armor that protects her from being approached by men and women. Or the chocolate gives a pleasant feeling and satisfies for a short time. After all, losing weight would only be satisfactory in the long term and requires effort and patience. This example can be applied to many situations. The intention behind every action is positive. But it is positive from the subjective point of view of the person and not necessarily from the point of view of society or outsiders.

4. Body, mind and soul are one system

NLP understands the body, the mind and the soul as a coherent system. This means in the opposite conclusion that the body can also influence soul and spirit and vice versa. Positive thoughts from the mind do the soul good and even influence the body. For example, a better posture and a positive, pleasant charisma could be among the consequences. It is always important that you keep this aspect in mind and do not try to look at body, soul and spirit separately. That doesn't work. For example, are you constantly ill? Then perhaps you should pay attention to your mind and soul. Stress and negative thoughts also attack the immune system and can lead to unpleasant results. Within the framework of self-coaching you can also work on these points and influence your mind positively. Sooner or later the body will also show changes in a positive direction.

5. We already have all the resources we need

Resources at this point mean experiences, pictures or existing knowledge. With this guiding principle, it should be noted that NLP assumes that every human being already has everything within him that is necessary to solve a problem. The resources are already available and only need to be activated. However, in many cases these resources are not or not yet available, we cannot simply access them. The techniques therefore serve in NLP to reveal exactly these necessary resources for problem solving. The goal is that after the exercises you can access your existing resources and solve the problems.

6. If something doesn't work, you have to try something else

Flexibility and a certain openness to alternatives are of great importance for the success of the development. This clearly applies to all techniques and ensures that you do not hold rigidly to an option. The techniques explained and implemented later in the book require a certain openness to new topics and views. It is not helpful to block directly against it and not try anything more. Rather, you should consider why you are trying these techniques before performing them. Often these techniques are used because the previous approach did not lead to the desired results. This is exactly why it is important to try something new and not stick to a known scheme F. That's why NLP is so interesting: There are many techniques with different approaches. If a technique doesn't work at all, you can achieve great success with others.

7. There are no mistakes or deficits within a communication, since all feedback is useful

This guiding principle fits in with the following sentence on the importance of communication. True or false is not given in the context of communication. The reason for this is that feedback is always required in communication. This feedback then shows whether the communication fits or should perhaps be adapted. You should therefore say goodbye quickly to the idea of wrong communication or deficits in communication. Feedback is therefore important because it is this feedback that really makes communication happen. There really is always feedback because silence is also a form of answer, a form that is often ignored.

8. The importance of communication is always the reaction to it

This is also an important guiding principle as it deals with the fundamental importance of and motivation behind communication. NLP assumes that communication is not based on the intention of the person writing or speaking. Rather, the meaning is only about the reaction to it. So it is not about what one person says but about how the other person understands it and how the environment reacts to it. When communicating, you must therefore always bear in mind that the reaction of your counterpart is important. So it is not so much about what you actually want to say. Rather, it is about the fact that your counterpart understands the pronounced thing. Think of the acceptance of the inner maps, which are constructed by experiences and versatile experiences. Because of this alone and the different perceptions, it is sometimes difficult to communicate in such a way that the content really reaches the other person.

9. The client's resistance is due to the consultant's lack of flexibility

If something doesn't work, you have to try something else. This applies not only to your own personality but also to the NLP consultant or the coach. It is very important to keep trying until a suitable solution is found because there are other techniques and possibilities that can lead to change. It is only crucial not to give up and show more flexibility. Every person can develop his or her personality. But some people need more patience than others.

10. If someone does something, this behavior can be imitated and passed on

What works for one person works for another. A behavior can therefore be duplicated. This is an advantage, for example, in things such as a successful sales strategy and should not be underestimated. NLP combines many different techniques and has been further developed over the years. This aspect is also important for success, as the techniques never actually work for just one person. Rather, it is important that a successful behavior or technique can be precisely analyzed and then copied. In this way, new insights can always be added to the existing ones.

At this point it should be noted that many techniques in NLP require a coach. So an external coach is ideal because the exercises alone are hardly or not at all convertible. But there are still many exercises that you can implement in self-coaching. Now we focus on these exercises. In a seminar with an NLP Coach there are many more techniques, which do not fit here because they are not suitable for self-coaching. The individual guiding principles also overlap and you will experience in the coming process what it is really about terms like an inner map. Because the theory of NLP alone is already interesting. But the techniques are only really helpful in practice and can lead to changes.

5. Start with small changes

Basically, it makes sense to start small and improve. This applies to all techniques within NLP. So don't start directly with the biggest problem but increase yourself bit by bit. Especially interesting in NLP are the techniques around anchoring and the linguistic pictures. The linguistic pictures represent a good option to bring about changes and to become aware of one's own behavior. You can dissolve fears and negative feelings and retrieve positive feelings. This provides you with resources that you would otherwise not have been able to access. At this point, however, there is an exercise that will make it easier for you to use the individual techniques afterwards. Because also for NLP in self-coaching you need a certain, pronounced imagination. Visual imagination particularly can be practiced in a targeted way and thus the following techniques can be implemented more easily.

Procedure for the exercise of visual imagination:

1. Imagine a fruit or a vegetable. For example an apple or paprika.

2. Now you should ask yourself some questions about the imaginary apple (or paprika). Some options are the following questions:

   o How far away is the fruit and how accurate is the representation? Is it a still image, is there movement?

   o Do you see more of a painting or a lifelike apple or pepper in 3D?

   o What color is the apple or pepper? Green, red, yellow?

   o What size is it in your imagination?

3. Start experimenting and playing with the image in your mind. Let the fruit get bigger or smaller; push it far away or bring it extremely close. There are many possibilities of imagination and change. In this way you train your visual imagination very effectively.

Use linguistic images sensibly

NLP's first guiding principle is that the map is not the territory. What sounds strange at first is actually a quite simple assumption, since according to NLP everyone has inner maps. These maps are used in certain situations and also protect us from stimulus flooding. An example would be the following situation: A friend tells you how she reacted to a certain remark from her boyfriend. You can't understand her reaction because you simply have a different opinion on the subject. Let's say it's about moving in together and you might think that moving in together after two years is way too early. Your girlfriend doesn't see it that way because she was influenced early on to move in together as early as possible and then to get married.

What at first sounds like a classic situation with different opinions is actually even more because in this situation your girlfriend falls back on her inner map about relationships and moving in together just like you do. But her boyfriend does exactly the same. Now the maps are quasi guides inside, which can be called up in certain situations. Everyone sees the world with his own eyes and has been shaped by many factors in the past and in the environment. But now the question arises whether this map is always correct and whether it cannot be changed. Since every person has formed this map and it is based on different experiences and assumptions, the map can also be outdated or simply inappropriate. On the basis of this assumption with the inner maps you can start with the technique of linguistic images. The existing maps are by no means unchangeable but can rather be adapted. Only the right technology is important. Of course, the awareness of the maps also plays a role.

This exercise is the right one for you, if:

- you always fall back on your inner scheme F in certain situations.

- you want to understand why exactly you see and understand a certain thing in the way you see and understand it.

- your prejudices or reactions in certain moments are quite typical for you.

- you feel that you are not responding rationally to one situation or another and your decisions are strongly influenced by your inner map.

- you want to deal with the topic of self-perception and external perception.

- self-reflection and a corresponding change are your goals.

- you want to modernize your inner maps in the long run.

The procedure of the linguistic images:

1. Imagine in the first moment a certain situation that occupies you. It is best to start with a rather small problem.

2. If you think about things in your life as well as about the future, you can also create two pictures matching the theme. This approach can be used, for example, in your professional situation before moving house or before questions about the partnership.

3. After the concrete idea or question you look for a suitable picture, which you connect with the situation. Usually a situation reminds you of certain things and you can now call them up.

4. Often not only one picture appears at the performance. Then it makes sense to allow the different images and select a suitable option according to your intuition. Normally one picture feels more fitting than another.

5. You are now working intensively on this presented picture. Therefore you should proceed creatively and not only write down everything. For example, you can buy and design a collage matching the picture in your head, a postcard or draw a picture. Leave your creativity free space because only in this way can you imagine the picture correctly and become aware of your inner maps.

6. Decorate your picture properly. Only then should you connect to your initial question. You can then ask yourself what this picture means and how you can connect it to your situation.

7. Concentrate on individual details in your picture. These little details have a meaning as well and are often left out of the picture.

The procedure using a practical example:

Let's call our example Martin. Martin is currently working as an online marketing manager in a medium-sized company in Cologne. But Martin is not satisfied; he feels constricted and would rather do another job today than tomorrow and move around the world. The following procedure is possible suitably to this initial situation:

1. First of all, Martin introduces himself to his current job situation. What is important at the moment and what is connected with the work?

2. Depending on the person the now appearing pictures are different. In this case, two images appear before the inner eye that fit the situation: One is a military barracks. The other picture is a cave system, which lets only a little light in. The association with the military is quite obvious and fits the feeling of imprisonment. For the exercise Martin chooses the image of the cave system, which extends in a landscape.

3. Martin now imagines the cave system in more detail and imagines it in his mind. Important questions would be, for example, Where is the cave system located? What is outside and how exactly does the landscape look like? What is inside the caves and what is the light like there? Are there perhaps stalactites, certain animals or plants or drawings on the walls? Is there a lake or river in the caves? How does the path run, is it straight or uneven? Are there other people and how far away are they? It is important to imagine the picture as accurately as possible and with many details.

4. Now it is about the further design of the picture. Collages, postcards and sketches are suitable for this. Remarks may appear and thoughts on individual places, plants and paths are precisely named. Martin is completely absorbed in the design of the picture with all details. The initial question is irrelevant in this process, since the attention is entirely on the picture.

5. The exercise concludes with an analysis of the image. Because this picture says a lot about your own thoughts and feelings, Martin notices two interesting things when he looks at the picture. First, there are many people in the cave and yet his own figure stands a little isolated and slightly apart in the corridor. The second fact is that the path winds for a long time and doesn't lead to a really recognizable goal. On the way there is a river, but otherwise there are no special points or destinations in the cave. Interesting is then a transfer of the picture to the presented initial question.

6. Now Martin can go even further and continue the thought of resigning and traveling around the world. A picture will certainly appear. This is to be painted then likewise and to be arranged exactly. Thus it is easier to recognize what exactly is connected with the thoughts and situations.

This example shows that an inner map exists. Because many others do the same work and are actually satisfied with it dissatisfaction is therefore not necessarily related to the work itself but to perception and to the inner map, the feeling in the situation, the feeling of being confined and the desire to break out is connected with things experienced. Another person would react differently. Nevertheless, the inner maps are not necessarily wrong; it is rather a matter of a different view of things and a subjective perception. For a change and for a better consciousness it is therefore very important that this map is recognized. The linguistic images not only help to uncover one's own resources but also show where there is still a need for action. Existing maps can, however, be replaced if they are no longer perceived as up to date or broken. It takes a little practice to implement the technique of the linguistic images or the images themselves. Then, however, valuable insights can be gained from the technique and it is possible to cause changes that way.

6. The technique of anchoring in NLP

Anchoring is without question the most important technique in NLP besides the later explained timeline. The aforementioned linguistic images with the inner map are also important, but with anchoring you can tie your feelings to certain things Or dissolve this connection. Have you ever heard of Pavlov's dog? This experiment can not only be heard in the lecture halls of social science and psychology students. Pavlov's dog was made to hear certain physical feelings at the sound of a bell. The stimulation of salivation by the expectation of food was probably the most important result. The Pavlov dog shows an important reaction, which we humans always have. When listening to a song, you see a situation in front of your inner eye. Maybe the cheerful song takes you back to this crazy summer or to a journey where the song was always played or the song is an anchor to a negative feeling, like heartache or the loss of a loved one. A certain smell catapults you to another place or in your mind to an experienced situation. The colorful picture on the wall evokes a feeling or the taste of cinnamon in your food takes you back to the past.

It's all quite normal, and it's almost the same as with Pavlov's dog because the feelings are connected with external stimuli. Smell, taste, hearing, seeing or feeling: What exactly is strongest for you depends on the type of dog. The interesting thing at this point is that you can make use of this form of anchor for your feelings. No wonder, then, that this technique is so indispensable in NLP and is used for personality development. The possibilities of anchoring techniques are extremely versatile and there are simple as well as advanced anchoring techniques. Many things of it you can acquire very well in self-coaching and thus work on your anchors. However, it is very helpful for creating new anchors if you know which influences have an effect on you, for example a song, a perfume, a spice or a picture. That actually varies from type to type and cannot be generalized.

You can take advantage of anchoring for various reasons:

- To dissolve existing anchors into negative feelings

- To create new anchors to positive feelings

- For conscious handling of the anchors and to

avoid unwanted anchors in the future

- For the recognition and control of existing anchors

- For better self-reflection and understanding of your anchors and feelings in certain situations

The famous experiment with the Pavlov dog was carried out in 1905. But even if you have never tried NLP before, or have studied sociology, you will still have anchors. After all, an anchor is nothing more than a reaction to a certain trigger. We humans associate such triggers with feelings. While one person associates positive feelings with a song, the next song may evoke the memory of the worst lovesickness in life. This is why it is so important to know one's own anchors and to acquire the knowledge to dissolve them or to create new ones, depending on exactly what the goal is. Cause and the unwanted effect ensure that an anchor exists here. So it is really always about cause and effect and about controlling these effects or reprogramming oneself, NLP does not mean neurolinguistic programming for nothing.

7. The procedure for creating a new anchor

You can create a new anchor in just a few steps. It rarely happens that you have to do the steps more than once. Depending on the anchor, it is often more difficult to solve an existing one than to create a new one. Important for this exercise, as for all other NLP techniques, is peace and quiet and a space in which you are undisturbed. Take some time for the exercise and do not do it under time pressure. After all, success should come.

1. Now choose a feeling you would like to anchor. This can be just about any feeling. It should be positive of course—because who wants to create negative anchors voluntarily?

2. When did you feel the desired feeling and what exactly happened in the situation? Imagine this situation intensively in front of your inner eye and imagine exactly how and when the feeling was created. Were you alone or were other people present? If so, who was present? The more you can imagine the feeling and the situation the better.

3. Strengthen the feeling by the exact memory and recall thereby in memory what you felt.

4. Enjoy the feeling and indulge in it. It is important that you experience this feeling strongly. Right now you are looking for an anchor for this feeling. What do you personally react most strongly to and which anchor works best for you? Maybe a smell or a song? Movements, sounds or pictures represent further possibilities. But it is important that you do not confuse your anchors with each other. So choose one that you don't use yet. Otherwise there will be a lot of chaos in your thoughts afterwards.

5. Now the whole thing is entering its interesting phase. Release your newly created anchor. What does it look like? Do you feel the desired feeling? If not, you should go through the previous steps a few more times until it works. It is basically easy to create a new anchor and then release it. Maybe you just need a little more patience and you need to imagine the situation and the feeling more precisely. In the future you can release the anchor as you wish.

An example in practice:

Our example person, Martin, has a number of anchors to show for himself—just like any normal person. But there are also feelings that are helpful in everyday life and not so easy to generate. About three years ago, Martin was almost 15 kilos lighter than he is today. Well-being is not necessarily a permanent condition and self-confidence also suffers, understandably. But it's really hard to stop eating and do more sports. What has happened to the wonderful feeling of lightness and well-being that made eating frustrated at the time completely unnecessary? The perfect example to create a new anchor and to create a positive feeling at any time! Are chips, beer and French fries still so appealing afterwards?

The procedure explained step by step:

1. Martin evokes the feeling of lightness that he always felt in his slimmer body at that time. This is a strong, positive feeling that has really inspired him.

2. When exactly was this feeling so intense and felt so good? Martin remembers this one party with his buddy where he had met a great

woman. The woman flirted with him and complimented him on his looks. The feeling of lightness was especially strong at this party and was burned into his memory. Martin calls the feeling and the whole situation very clearly in front of his eyes. What did the room look like, which people were still present and what music was played?

3. Now he strengthens the feeling through this precise idea and recalls it correctly.

4. Martin indulges in the feeling of lightness and feels this feeling flowing through his body. His body actually feels lighter at this very moment and the positive feeling is really strong and beautiful. But Martin still needs an anchor and has noticed that he reacts very strongly to songs. With certain songs he connects memories and often feels transported back to a completely different place and time. Of course it is obvious to use a song as an anchor. Martin chooses a song that was played at the party and is positively charged for him. The first bars of the song are now his anchor and are strongly connected with the feeling of lightness.

5. Now it's about the test phase. Martin turns on the song he has chosen as his anchor. And lo and behold: It worked because the feeling of lightness is suddenly present and just feels good. So it's no longer so easy to fall back on fast food when you're frustrated with your current body. So the mission has been successful and the new, positive anchor is certainly not wrong and still easy to retrieve.

A suitable anchor must be selected depending on the type. This does not have to be a song or a tone. A picture or smell are also suitable. With self-coaching and with the independent setting of anchors it is not quite so easy to use touch as an anchor, since you would need another person for it. The suitable setting of the anchor is, however, very important. Anchors such as a handshake or a hug are unsuitable since they are often triggered in our culture. Setting such an anchor requires a lot of patience and it is better to go for less obvious triggers. By the way, there are no limits to the fantasy of positive feelings. Motivation, self-confidence, focus, energy, lightness or happiness—these are just a few options. That is exactly the reason why anchoring is so popular and comes preferentially in the personality development to the employment.

8. Advanced Anchors: Stacked and Collapsing Anchors

The method explained above can be described as simple anchoring. It is a technique that with a little patience and practice is quite easy to use. But what exactly happens when you need to trigger multiple resources in a situation? In seminars, job interviews or on a first date, self-confidence, positive charisma and confidence are meaningful feelings. But a single anchor is not enough for that, so advanced technology is popular. The technique is known in English as the stacked anchor. The stacked anchors ensure that you can access not only one feeling but various positive feelings when releasing the respective anchor. You can use the steps above to do this. However, it is important to stack different emotions on a single anchor. In this way it is possible to feel all feelings by releasing an anchor. But it is definitely an advanced technique because it requires more patience.

This is how you proceed:

1. What feelings do you want to trigger? Examples would be self-confidence, focus or a positive charisma.

2. Now you begin, as described before, to set the anchors for the feelings. All desired feelings are to be set on a single anchor.

3. In any case, choose a strong anchor and use a song, a sequence of notes, pictures or a scent. The exact anchor is again strongly related to your own type.

4. In this situation you trigger all feelings through the stacked anchors and can access all resources at once. This procedure is also very popular in seminars on NLP.

Resolving and Replacing Negative Anchors

The collapsing anchors mentioned above are another advanced technique in NLP. Suppose you don't want to have a negative anchor anymore and want to use a positive anchor for it. Then it's about collapsing or collapsing an anchor. This technique may not be so easy, but with a little patience it can be learned as well. This way you can effectively free yourself from negative anchors and retrieve resources. You can create several steps at once and can free yourself from blockades. This anchor is known as Collapsing Anchor.

In this way you dissolve negative anchors:

1. In the first step, you need a negative anchor that you want to resolve. This can be a reaction to an event as well as a very strong memory of a negative experience. Remember exactly when this anchor is triggered with what feeling.

2. For this technique you need not only one anchor but two. But this other anchor must be connected with a positive feeling like perhaps

joy, happiness or euphoria. The positive anchor must be very strong for the exercise to succeed.

3. Now it gets exciting: In the first step you trigger the negative anchor. Then you trigger the positive anchor.

4. Always release both anchors alternately. The distances are getting shorter and shorter, so you definitely need a little patience.

5. Now it is a matter of dissolving the negative and the positive anchor at the same time.

6. How do you feel about it and what exactly happens inside you? You collapse the anchors and actually manage to dissolve a negative anchor.

It is quite normal that this technique requires a moment of time and does not work immediately. After all, the first thing that has to work is for the anchors to collapse, and that's not possible in a minute. But this way you can dissolve negative anchors and don't have to deal with them in the future.

9. The timeline: How the past and the future influence the present

A popular technique suitable for self-coaching is the use of the timeline. The timeline helps you to identify your own resources. But the timeline can do much more and also shows some interesting things. It's all about the sense of time. Have you ever noticed that time feels different for everyone? Of course there is measurable time. Our watches show seconds, minutes, hours and even days. But just because a day has 24 hours does not mean that every day is the same. For some, the day goes by like a flight, and for others, a day lasts a week. What is the reason for this? Now, time is subjective and we feel time just like we perceive smells, a taste or pictures as well as music. Everyone feels things differently because perception is related to the five senses.

Basically, the perception of time is linked to the things one experiences in time. To stay with our example person Martin: Martin has now taken a month off and is on the road in South America. On one day he climbs a volcano and gets to know many people, enjoys the time out, takes unforgettable pictures and has to make a lot of effort while hiking. This day is felt to be very long and is also stored in the memory in a completely different way than it would be the case with a classic office day. Because the office day is as tough as chewing gum and often flies away anyway, especially when there is nothing to do in the evening other than a film. The personally experienced time is therefore always linked to the experiences during this period.

A distortion of the time into a special length or the feeling that the time is very short is strongly influenced by different things. Only some of these influencing factors are:

- Uniformity or variety of activity

- The number of events or the amount of information received

- The nature of the experience or events so pleasant or less pleasant things

- The activity level in time

- Flow. This refers to the condition at work or during sport, which allows us to merge completely into an activity. Flow strongly distorts the perception of time.

But now, at the thought of the timeline, it is added that time does not only correspond to a subjective feeling. Rather, we humans tend to store our experiences in a chronological form or in a timeline. This is also perfectly normal, so that memories are often stored in a kind of line or chain. Before experience C there is experience B and before that is experience A. Not all things are stored in the same way so that long office days almost disappear from memory at some point. Quite often this storage occurs unconsciously and it is important to become aware of this process. By the way, not only past things are saved in the timeline! Future and planned events are also part of this chain and also make up the human being.

Timeline therapy has been used at NLP since the 1970s. For this there are different options of the procedure. Since, according to many experts, we are the sum of our memories in life, it makes sense to start here. Because all experiences in the present and in the future are shaped by what we have experienced according to this assumption. A person with an accident in the mountains will experience a hike differently than a person who can do long tours without any problems. Fear finds its key in experiences and we do not always keep these things in mind. In addition, it should be noted that there is a conscious part of a personality next to the unconscious part. The subconscious also has a lot to say and also makes a person. As a basic assumption, for example, it is important to recognize that a man who grew up in an upper middle class in Germany has completely different experiences and ideas than a person from a third-world country. A woman from poorer backgrounds in Morocco or Mexico has a really different view of things. This can be explained not only by cultural differences but also by experiences. That's why the timeline and corresponding exercises are so interesting because they can really make a difference.

This exercise is about walking or hovering over an imaginary timeline. In this way, fears and oppressive feelings can also be resolved. In self-coaching this approach is not suitable for people who have serious psychological problems. Then timeline therapy is also possible but should definitely only be used under the supervision of a therapist. The easiest way is to imagine the individual events strung on a string or pearl necklace. The last experience or event is then based on other experiences on the pearl necklace. It is even easier for some people to imagine the present, past or future as a vehicle.

For example, you are in a car on a road. Everything behind you is the past, the path in front of you is the future and the current location is your present. Some people now find it easier to imagine these things spatially and others have more difficulties with it. Try to imagine exactly this car or imagine that the experiences in your life are lined up on a string of pearls. Which idea is easier now also depends on the respective type. It is therefore not always possible to name the perfect option as a whole, since every person is a little different again.

The exercise suits you if:

- you sometimes feel strong negative feelings like fear, anger or jealousy.

- you often feel trapped in a feeling and cannot get out of your skin or react differently.

- your feelings are hindering you in certain situations.

- you find that these feelings have a negative impact on friendships, relationships or professional success.

- you react very impulsively in certain situations and more or less go up in the air.

- you simply cannot forgive some people for their actions and these feelings burden you.

- the past influences you so strongly with the experiences in the present that social interaction seems difficult. Maybe that's why you can't have longer relationships.

- You show downright neuroses in some respects. For example the panic fear of dirt or small rooms.

Procedure of the Timeline Exercise:

1. First look for a feeling that burdens you. It can be a feeling like anger, fear, shame or jealousy. Often such a feeling occurs in certain situations and then burdens you enormously. Think carefully when this feeling is particularly strong and in which situations it is less strong.

2. Now you recall an experience where this feeling was particularly strong. When exactly was that? What happened in that situation? Which physical reactions do you feel and how strong are these? For example, it could be a dull feeling in your stomach or a tightness in your throat.

3. Now we come to your personal timeline. Imagine time as a street or a river. Where exactly is the past and where is the future? The question may sound banal, but not everyone has the same spatial idea. Is the past right or left of you? Or rather behind you? Imagine this timeline very precisely and figuratively.

4. Now hover in thought above this timeline. You should be able to float very high and just recognize the road. Imagine the individual events of the past in the form of pearls or boxes that are on this line.

5. Now go back on this line and follow your feeling. When exactly did you feel the feeling for the first time? Before or after the birth? Try to name the time when your subconscious

saved exactly this experience.

6. Recognize the experience that triggered your feelings. Now concentrate on a positive learning effect. Every experience has such a learning effect to offer and this should be absolutely positive. Remember this learning's effect consciously.

7. Now go a little further back on your personal timeline to a moment before this experience. Everything was still good and you didn't even know what to expect. The negative feelings come only in the future. Look at this future and listen to yourself. It is very important to let go of the feelings at this point. In many cases this doesn't work from the beginning. Let go of the feelings bit by bit.

8. The aim is to deal with the situation neutrally. However, this also means that you no longer show any physical reaction to the original situation. With a little practice you can always let go of negative feelings and release blockages.

9. Only after you have let go of the feelings do you float back to the present.

The **most difficult** thing about this exercise for most people is **letting go of their feelings**. Returning to the origin of negative feelings or blockages is usually not the problem. In any case, it is not the main problem. It is very important in timeline therapy that positive learning effects are used. Only if the subconscious mind is sufficiently charged with these learning effects can the negative feelings be released. Imagine that the feelings fall away from you and disappear. The more pictorial your imagination is, the better this letting go usually works. A good supplementary exercise is also a test to see if the procedure has worked. Follow the first steps and go back to the experience in your timeline. What exactly does this experience trigger in you now? If you have succeeded in the exercise correctly, you should no longer feel any negative feelings. Do you still feel anger, fear or another negative feeling? Then you should do the exercise again if possible. Little by little the handling of the triggering situation becomes better.

A practical example:

Let's stay with our example person Martin. Because Martin has a big problem with jealousy and often difficulties to get away with it, a feeling is not innate and is therefore a good example. But it would also be similar with feelings like anger or fear. We are not born with it, but the experiences in the course of time make sure that these feelings occur in certain moments. This also makes it difficult for the time being to get to the bottom of it. So Martin is jealous and therefore had a lot of problems in his last relationship. The relationship didn't end because of jealousy, but this feeling clearly didn't simplify the partnership. Now Martin introduces himself to his personal timeline. For him, the past is on the line to his left and the future is on his right.

His approach to the exercise:

1. Martin imagines the feeling of jealousy and a situation when this feeling was so strong the last time.

2. This last situation also leads to physical reactions. The heart beats faster in anger and Martin feels a tightness in his throat. He also

feels a lump of anger and fear in his stomach at the thought of memory. So the memory can be felt physically.

3. Then Martin visualizes his personal timeline as a street. On this street there are the experiences and events in the form of boxes, which are parked.

4. Now Martin floats mentally far above the road in the air. The boxes take on the size of pebbles and the road can only be seen as a line in the landscape. Perhaps the boxes still glow slightly and the last event is highlighted. Because the performance differs a little from each other.

5. Now Martin goes back in the street of his memory to the actual cause of the feelings. He relies completely on his feelings and his subconscious because the subconscious knows exactly where the cause can actually be found.

6. Now the question about the time is important: Was it before or after the birth? What sounds esoteric actually works. Even in the womb certain things can be felt very strongly and can

be retrieved. Martin knows immediately that the cause of the jealousy has happened after birth. It's even more accurate: the feeling is due to an experience at the age of four.

7. Martin remembers: When he was four years old, there was another sibling and his brother was born. The strong feeling can be traced back to the first months of his brother's life, who was initially very ill and demanded a lot of attention from his parents.

8. After realizing the event, Martin perceives his feelings and tries to charge his subconscious to a positive experience. There is a positive learning experience to every experience. Even if sometimes this is just the fact that you have survived and become stronger. Martin realizes that the love of his parents and especially that of his mother had not diminished at all. It was just his feeling because his brother needed so much attention at that time.

9. Now Martin floats a little further back on his timeline in front of this experience. When everything was still good and the feeling of

jealousy was unknown or at least not known to this extent. Then Martin looks into the future and lets go of the negative feelings. At this point the feeling of jealousy with all its physical side effects has disappeared. This is less surprising now, since at this point the incisive experience had not yet taken place.

10. The feeling is now neutral and Martin floats back into the present. The straining feelings and the physical reaction have disappeared. Martin no longer feels the strong feeling of jealousy because he has dissolved the negative feelings of the cause. Others need longer and have to let go of the negative feelings bit by bit. In the end, the feeling should be neutralized because the subconscious has been positively charged.

For the implementation of the exercise you therefore need a little patience, a strong and unpleasant feeling and the will to dive into negative emotions. The timeline exercise is not pleasant and beautiful, but it can release blockages and fears. You will need some imagination, but then it is possible to do the exercise. What feeling is it with you? What is it that weighs you down or burdens you again and again? Such a feeling is present in most people and represents a good starting point for the exercise. Use the exercise only if you want to influence your feelings and react differently in the future. Surely it is necessary to do the self-coaching exercise more than once in order to achieve really visible results.

10. The Timeline exercise is so difficult - why?

However, the exercise of the timeline is quite a profound affair. In addition, every human being has one or two senses, which are preferably used in perception. In keeping with this, visualizing the timeline is not easy for everyone, and for some it can be a real challenge to do this exercise. Therefore, there are some aspects to consider when using the timeline technique. For the best results, you should consider the following:

- Always do the exercise in a quiet room where nobody will interrupt you.

- Sometimes very intense internal resistance occurs during the timeline exercise. You should respect these and not touch them during self-coaching. Often such resistance is due to a trauma and the body uses these resistances for protection. The mechanism is useful and it can be very painful if you go against it.

- Always go step by step. The timeline must first be completely visualized before the processing of the experiences and feelings can begin. It is important that you do not mix these two things, because only then are really good results possible.

- Since there are different types of perception, it is important to really imagine the timeline very precisely. Make sure it's not too dark or blurry, and don't focus on sounds or shapes. With enough concentration, each type can visualize a timeline in front of the inner eye.

- Practice regularly the inner visualization of different things. These inner images are always very important in NLP exercises. With a little practice you will get better and better with the exact implementation. Then it will also be easier to achieve the corresponding results.

10.1 Present, past and future have an effect

Finally, there is another interesting point concerning the technique of the timeline. Not only the present and the past influence you and your reactions. Also the future finds its place in the timeline. Maybe you have already thought so intensely about the future that these worries and feelings have strongly influenced your behavior in the present. This is exactly what is meant by the aspect of the future in the timeline. The exercise of dissolving the past is not only possible on this path of the timeline. Floating into the future and dissolving fears is also possible. This procedure is always recommended when certain things in the future trigger such negative feelings. You can only fully utilize your resources and bring the best results in the present if you are not blocked by the future.

10.2 The voices in my head

Do you know this ugly, always very critical voice in your head? If not, you probably have a lot of self-confidence or simply no self-doubt. Normally we humans have this voice in our heads in certain situations and it's really not very friendly. No matter if the voice says "you idiot," "you really can't do anything," or "how do you look again? - it does not make you happy. However, you can take the power away from your critical inner voice and reduce the negative effect significantly. This is the effect of this technique, which has become very popular with NLP.

This technique is suitable for you:

- if you often hear critical voices in the interior.

- if you are plagued by self-doubt.

- when your inner voices and doubts are blocking you.

- if you have only little confidence in yourself and you slow down again and again.

- if you can't get negative sentences from other people out of your head.

Take power from the inner voice:

1. In the first step you imagine the voice very exactly, which harasses you again and again. Then you have to consciously change this voice and take its power away from it. Which voice do you hear again and again? Maybe it is your own voice, that of your mother-in-law or

that of your boss. It's different for everyone, but all voices have one thing in common: they block and unsettle you. Imagine the voice as exactly as possible: What does it say and what is the sound like?

2. In your thoughts you now change the sound of the imaginary voice. It is definitely funny and helpful to imagine the voice in the sound of Mickey Mouse, Donald Duck or another comic figure. Or what if the voice of your boss suddenly sounds childish, like a voice break or like an eccentric woman off track? There are no limits to your imagination. Does it already work and does the voice lose its effect in the squeaky Mickey Mouse sound?

3. It doesn't always work to take power from the voice with a different sound. Another very good option is to change the speaking speed. Slow down the voice in your imagination. Maybe as if a record is playing slower and slower. Or accelerate the voice so that it almost flips over and is barely understandable. How does that feel? Does the voice have the same power over you as before?

4. Another option is to change the direction of the voice. Imagine the voice coming from above like from heaven, from below or from behind. Is there a direction where you perceive the voice less intensely? The muffled voice like from the underground may have a lesser effect than the voice that talks you in front of you. Here, too, you have to test the different options and find the best one.

5. What works best for you? Voice or speech itself, speed or direction? Every person is different and therefore needs appropriate solutions so that the voice inside loses power. But let's be honest; the voice of the always angry and critical boss sounds less threatening inside as Mickey Mouse, doesn't it?

Switch off the voices in practice:

Our example person, Martin, has a job that he doesn't really enjoy. But this is not only due to the lack of freedom and the work itself. Another big problem is his choleric boss, who has probably never heard of personnel management or empathy. Even after work and sometimes in a meeting, Martin thinks he can still hear the boss's voice, which calls him a failure, incapable or a fool. That's why Martin is now taking targeted action against the power of the inner voices and doing the above exercise.

This is how Martin proceeds:

1. First of all, he imagines the voice of his angry boss. She says, "You really are completely incapable!" Martin feels bad; the voice in his head has a lot of power over him and creates strong self-doubt.

2. Now he changes the sound of the voice and imagines the words in Mickey Mouse art. The performance works pretty well and makes sure that the voice doesn't seem so powerful anymore.

3. But Martin goes one step further: the Mickey Mouse voice slows down in his head and distorts the sound further. Now the voice doesn't sound like the angry boss anymore. He performs this performance several times until

it is quite easy to imagine the voice as a squeaky and distorted comic voice.

4. Now Martin has to make sure he doesn't start laughing when his boss insults or criticizes him in the future because the idea of the squeaking comic voice can be quite intense.

11. Effectively resolve fears and phobias: The Fast Phobia Cure

Just like anchoring or the timeline, the Fast Phobia Cure is one of the classic techniques in NLP. Actually everyone has fears and phobias unless he or she has been intensively involved with personality development for a long time. What about you? What makes you afraid and do you perhaps even have a phobia that has made your life difficult for you more than once? The fear of failure, the fear of being alone or the real panic when it comes to heights, elevators, narrow rooms, darkness or spiders; fears can occur in many areas and cause a feeling of paralysis. That is why it is so important to dissolve these fears and phobias as much as possible and to go through life more freely. The technique reminds one a little of collapsing anchors and makes sure that you lose your fear. However, it is also rather an advanced technique and nothing that beginners in NLP directly create. Be patient and train your imagination.

This exercise suits you if:

- you feel anxiety in certain situations and want to eliminate it.

- phobias often make life difficult for you.

- you sometimes feel paralyzed or panic-stricken.

- you want to be freer and access your resources without blocking them.

Fighting fears and phobias step by step:

1. Imagine a cinema hall inside you that is completely empty. Sit down mentally and look towards the screen.

2. Now you clearly recall an image that was still before the situation that triggered your fear. It is supposed to be a picture on the cinema screen where everything is still good and safe.

3. As in the timeline exercise, you now float upwards in the cinema auditorium and see yourself from above. You should see yourself from the outside as a spectator looking at the

screen.

4. Now make sure that the images on the screen lose their color and are displayed like an old black-and-white movie. You keep the view from above on your person and allow the frightening picture to show. Maybe there's a giant spider, a snake or a very dark, narrow room. Let these images run until the frightening situation is over.

5. Now float back into your own person in the auditorium and stay with the picture when the frightening situation runs over again.

6. Now you turn on the colors again in your imagination and rewind the film extremely fast. Arrive at the situation that took place before the frightening situation.

7. Make sure that the canvas becomes white or blurred in thought.

8. Repeat the previous steps several times faster and faster.

9. Now play the movie several times and make sure that it is played very fast. This way you can neutralize the frightening situation.

10. With enough practice and the imagination of the cinema, you will gradually lose your fear or phobia.

Putting it into practice

Not only was Martin afraid of his choleric boss, there are many more phobias and fears that need to be resolved step by step. Martin's phobia of spiders, which only recently completely destroyed him in the bathroom with an eight-legged roommate, is particularly distressing. The elimination of the fear of spiders is therefore in the foreground and is not easy in any case. After all, the phobia is quite pronounced and hasn't only existed recently.

1. Martin introduces himself to the previously explained scene with the cinema hall. He sees himself in his favorite cinema, sitting quite far back with a clear view of the big screen.

2. Shortly before he saw the spider in the bathroom, he was in the living room watching a movie and indulging in a beer. So everything was fine. He concentrates very firmly on this picture and projects it in his mind onto the cinema screen.

3. Thanks to the timeline technique, Martin knows exactly how he imagines himself to float above a situation or, in this case, a person. That's exactly what he's doing now, floating in thought above his sitting self. At the same time he switches off the colors and ensures that his projected image is only visible in black and white.

4. In this view from above he looks at the canvas and now winds the story forward to the unpleasant confrontation. The spider with all its hairy legs appears clearly visible on the cinema screen. But Martin looks from above and not frontally at the picture, which has also lost power due to the lack of color. It doesn't feel so frightening anymore.

5. At this point, the film continues on the big screen until the moment when his roommate catches the spider, stops it and it disappears. Then everything is fine again.

6. After witnessing this good end, after the frightening situation, Martin now leaves the screen and slips back into his me. Then he lets the film rewind in fast motion back to the point on the couch with the beer and the film.

7. In thought he makes everything white and repeats the previous steps again and again. Each time his fear of the spider is a little smaller. Then he starts to fast-forward and rewind the film again and again.

8. The exercise is done and even if the phobia of spiders is not completely defeated yet, the animals seem much more harmless. With a little more practice Martin will be able to stop being afraid in a few weeks. He hasn't met a Tarantula yet, but even that can become easier in the future.

The technique at hand is indeed very well suited to reducing fears and phobias. However, you should be aware that you have to face your fears for this exercise. In the beginning that requires really overcoming and it is then perhaps not so simple. It also always depends on the strength of the fear, how difficult it is to reduce it or even make it disappear. In any case, regular practice and the will to achieve this change is helpful. After all, there is no point in holding on to one's own fears. At this point it is also important to realize that the inner images determine our feelings very strongly. Thus they also determine our fears and can change if the underlying inner images are changed. This is exactly what you need to achieve through technique and practice.

12. The magic circle: solves fears and problems

Another popular technique at NLP is the magic circle, which is used to solve fears and problems. The magic circle is a circle on the ground that you imagine. Inside the circle there is a force field, which supports you and helps you with the problem. Therefore, the technique strongly reminds one of anchoring but is carried out from a different motivation. Within the circle there is your anchor and you activate motivation and self-confidence. This helps you to solve problems and overcome fears.

This exercise suits you if:

- you are looking for support for anxiety and problem-solving.

- a short time-out and inner recharging with positive feelings in difficult moments helps you.

- you want to access your hidden resources to deal with problems.

- you want to get to know yourself better and you want to have positive feelings.

Step by step to the powerful magical circle:

1. Stand or sit in a quiet room with a free area in front of you on the floor. Visualize a circle in front of you on the floor.

2. Now shape your circle appropriately in your imagination. At the end the circle should be a place filled with self-confidence, peace and positive energy. How exactly do you imagine such a circle? Consider colors, a border and a possible fill color. The exact details always depend on the respective type because for everyone security and confidence are connected with other colors or forms.

3. Similar to anchoring, it is now a matter of imagining a situation in which you feel particularly self-confident. Confidence in your abilities, positive energy and the certainty that every problem can be solved—these are exactly the things you should remind yourself of now. Imagine the positive situation very intensively.

4. The positive feeling is now very strong? Perfect, then you can step forward and enter your magical circle. Let the feelings fill you.

5. As soon as you realize that your feeling is getting weaker, you leave your imaginary circle.

6. Now comes a new technology that is popular in NLP: the separator. This means that you simply distract yourself for a moment and engage in something completely different. This briefly brings you into a neutral state.

7. Wait about one or maybe two minutes and then enter the magic circle again. In the best case you feel the positive feelings when entering the circle. If this is not yet the case, don't despair. Repeat the previous steps several times until you also feel the feeling when entering the circle.

8. The magic circle is now an anchor in which there are positive feelings. Are you afraid or very insecure because of a problem? Imagine your newly created magic circle and step into

it. Thanks to the positive feelings inside, the fear shrinks and a problem is no longer so unsolvable.

A practical example of the circle:
From time to time in Martin's job, just as in his private life, there are these situations that trigger fears. Or there are simply problems that seem enormous and can hardly be solved at first glance. With the magic circle, Martin mentally moves to a safe, positive place that helps a lot in overcoming the problems. This is how he proceeds with the creation:

1. He imagines a magic circle and imagines it inwardly. In Martin's imagination, the circle is reminiscent of one of the magical stone circles found in so many places in Scotland. Mighty, weathered stones stand slightly crooked around a circle with juicy green grass and some wild flowers growing in the middle. The performance is very lively.

2. Now Martin imagines the positive feelings of self-confidence, inner strength and positive energy he felt during his last salary negotiation. He intensifies the feeling and lets

these positive feelings flow through his whole body.

3. The feelings are really very strong just at that moment he enters his personal magical stone circle.

4. Now he steps out and briefly distracts himself with the thoughts of something else.

5. The exercise didn't work immediately, which is really normal. After the fourth scenario Martin feels the positive feelings inside the magic circle.

6. With existing fears and problems he now enters his imaginary magic circle and strengthens himself through the feelings anchored there.

13. Pacing and Leading: Adaptation to our interlocutors

Again and again NLP talks about Pacing and Leading. This is a technique that benefits salespeople in particular and is helpful in communication. You have certainly experienced salespeople who behave a little like chameleons and are always ready to talk to the right person, haven't you? However, this is not only about adjusting to the person you are talking to but also about a technique that is well known in NLP under the name of Pacing and Leading. The point is that you adapt your body language to your conversation partner. Originally, the terms have become known as submission and dominance. However, this does not quite correspond to the meaning meant here. It is more about aligning and leading. Through the alignment you are able to communicate better with your counterpart and can be accepted into a group much easier. But when exactly does the technique really benefit you?

Use Pacing and Leading when:

- you want to persuade your interlocutor to do certain things like make a purchase.

- you want to gain important insights about yourself and your own actions.

- you want to make it easier for yourself to integrate into new groups or in a foreign environment.

- you want to get in touch with your interlocutor and give him exactly this impression.

- you are interested in good communication and want to be successful in this way.

Procedure for Pacing and Leading

1. Find someone to talk to. This can be any person. However, it makes sense not to use this exercise necessarily as the first exercise in a very important customer meeting.

2. Before you go to leading, you have to do the pacing. To do this, you need to be fully attuned to the person you are talking to. Mirror body language, facial expression, breathing and speaking speed. Repeat the last things with the same words and use the same movements in

this case. There are a number of levels where Pacing is practicable. First concentrate on all things that happen on the non-verbal level. Only then do you move on to the verbal level.

3. At the end you should mirror your conversation partner and adjust to them. In many cases, lovers and children unconsciously perform pacing and use the tactics successfully. This is because this process is quite normal when you are interested in the other person.

4. Only when you have completely managed to successfully pace your interlocutor and have a good basis for communication can you move on to leading. Pacing takes time and that is perfectly normal. So take the necessary time to perform the technique.

5. Now it's on to the leading. However, you should be aware that leading requires respect and prudence. Don't try to force your conversation partner to do things. After all, it is a subtle and not extremely strong influence. In the state of pacing, start by slightly changing

your non-verbal language. A change in posture, movement or facial expression are some examples.

6. At this point you will also notice whether you were successful in pacing. Only then will your conversation partner adapt their facial expressions and gestures to suit you.

7. Now you can easily influence and steer your conversation partner. The previously described report is important for this. In addition, your approach should be gentle and not abrupt. Then the person you are talking to will feel comfortable while leading and will not feel negatively influenced or manipulated.

The technique in practice:

Martin makes it easy for himself in this case and first observes children on the playground next to his apartment. This makes it much easier to use the right approach and recognize the potential of pacing and leading. The technique is suitable for self-coaching but always requires a different person. However, the other person does not need to know that such an exercise is taking place. It is easier to first observe such a technique in others and then perform it yourself.

1. Martin sits on the bench in the evening and watches the children play. He immediately notices that new children imitate others. Same movements, same games and an adaptation to the already present children on site. After some time, the child is accepted into the group and a joint game takes place. Pacing can therefore be observed everywhere and does not look so difficult at first glance.

2. Then Martin looks for an opportunity to use it. The option arises when his roommate wants to sit down with him with a beer and something to eat. The communication between the two isn't always ideal and Martin would like to tell his roommate that he could help a little bit more with cleaning the apartment. It often looks very chaotic.

3. So he begins to mirror his roommate non-verbally at first. He imitates gestures and posture and adapts as much as possible to his roommate's rhythm of breathing. Then the

facial expression is added. Not so easy because there are many little things to consider. In addition the interlocutor should not feel like a monkey. It is therefore important to proceed cautiously and take time at this point.

4. The non-verbal adaptation worked after some time. Now he is almost overwhelmed because now also a verbal adaptation is added. Of course he does not imitate all words because the desired effect is not achieved. Rather, he repeats a few words and thus represents the report piece by piece.

5. In this phase Martin easily changes his gestures and posture. His roommate changes the same things and reflects him. The leading phase has begun and he begins to gently steer the conversation. He focuses on the cleanliness of the apartment.

6. In the end, the experiment has worked and the apartment will be a little tidier and cleaner in the future. There will be no quarrels or problems afterwards as a feeling of well-being clearly prevails.

14. Manipulation: Desirable or not?

Perhaps you already suspect that anchoring, just like the other techniques, is not a completely harmless tool. Anchoring has become known through sects like Scientology, for example. It is definitely a useful and useful exercise. But the combination of the cause with the undesirable effect is also suitable for abuse. A little caution is therefore appropriate. It is for good reason that anchoring feelings or certain reactions is also a topic that can be found in many thrillers. All in all, it is always best if you know these possibilities and are intensively occupied with them. Thus protection against such unwanted manipulations is rather possible. Very often coaches use such anchors in seminars on NLP, which are then called up later. It's an effective tool when it comes to demonstrating the effect of NLP. But this should also call for at least a little caution when playing with the subconscious. In this way you consciously set anchors and dissolve unwanted anchors.

An example from my own experience, which is not quite so negative but only a bit annoying, comes here. Biology lessons, eighth or ninth grade. The teacher told the pupils a story about a man who harassed girls in a school. One day, the man hanged himself under the roof because the girls were following him. It was precisely these girls who were involved in the production of a song and sang along to the chorus of the song. The chorus contains the statement, "Get him, get him under the roof." The man of the story simply couldn't stand it any longer and therefore took his own life. Pink Floyd's song may not be on the radio as often as it used to be—but when it is, the subconscious jumps on and this verse can be heard. Completely unconscious and the first time this message caused quite a shock. Of course the words are not audible to anyone but me and the whole song is in English. No words at all in German. Of course the sentence is not built into the chorus. But it's not that easy to convey that to your subconscious. This example should only make it clear that the anchors can be used specifically for demonstrations. But to get rid of them is not that easy. Whether it is a certain memory, a feeling or a message: Many things are possible with an anchor.

What applies to anchoring is also applicable to the other techniques. NLP offers powerful and very effective tools. You can release your personal resources, unfold yourself and achieve a lot in connection with the exercises. Less fear, less negative feelings and more motivation in everyday life. These things should be emphasized in any case. But it is very important not to lose sight of the other side. This should above all mean that you should carry out NLP in self-coaching with caution. Do not force your mind to work with a severe trauma itself. Don't throw any other person into problems and don't set anchors that will cause difficulties afterwards. Because NLP brings very powerful methods with it, the way to self-coaching is of interest. You can influence yourself in terms of how far you want to go. A seminar with a coach should therefore be chosen carefully and in the best case a well-known and successful coach. Otherwise there may be less desirable side effects when traveling to your own self.

15. Conclusion

In summary, NLP is definitely not just a single technique or a method. NLP is a collection of methods and not every technique is suitable for every person. In addition, which technique is most useful always depends on the situation. The fact that many processes and behaviors are controlled quite unconsciously is now well known. More important at this point, however, is that these things are not irrevocably fixed but can be changed. This is often possible as with the previous techniques in self-coaching. However, the techniques for self-coaching are more about general problems and classical behavior. For profound psychological problems it is important to consult a therapist because not everything can be treated by yourself. A little caution with one's own feelings and subconsciousness is therefore appropriate.

This book will help you to release blockages and negative feelings. In addition, the techniques presented are suitable for the new anchoring of positive feelings and for accessing one's own resources. Because all resources are already present in you, it is only about releasing or activating them. This assumption belongs to the principles of NLP and is just as important as the existing maps and the positive intention of all people. NLP is often taught in seminars by a coach. However, the methods described in this book show you that self-coaching is also a very effective approach. The linguistic pictures and simple anchors are particularly suitable for beginners. Then you can try the timeline and the advanced anchors. In this way you release your resources and manage to escape from disturbing and stressful behaviors and feelings.

Paul Edelmaier

Legal notice and imprint